Student Information

Name: _____

Grade: _____

Teacher: _____

Parent/Guardian: _____

Parent/Guardian: _____

Counselor: _____

Allergies: _____

Bus Number: _____

My Writing Affirmation:
I Can Write! I Will Write! I Am Writing!

Class Schedule

Period	Time	Subject	Teacher

Writing to Respond
Practice and Assessment
3-5

Martha Joseph Watts, Ed.D

Aunty Marcella

Buddinwriters Academy LLC

Florida, United States of America

Writing to Respond: Practice and Assessment Grades 3-5

Copyright 2015, 2020 © Buddinwriters Academy LLC
ISBN: 978-1-7333511-2-6
Rev. Date 04/15/2020

All rights reserved. No part of this book may be reproduced or transmitted in any form or by any means, electronic or mechanical, including photocopying or recording, or by any information storage and retrieval system, without permission in writing from the copyright owner.

This is a workbook that complements the Writing to Respond: Cultivating Habits (2013) text. It introduces students to evidence-based writing, and it serves as a place for parent or school educators to monitor students' writing progress.

Cover illustrations are from previously published works of Buddinwriters Academy LLC.

This book was printed in the United States of America.

To order additional copies or for additional information:
Buddinwriters Academy LLC
buddinwriters@gmail.com or
www.buddinwriters.com

Putting it all Together – Practice 4

Create your own title and write your paragraph

_____

_____

_____

_____

_____

_____

_____

_____

_____

_____

_____

_____

_____

Self-Check: Ask yourself: Did I …	Yes or Not Yet	Teacher
…identify and name the author and title of the article or story?		
…summarize or use two sentences to tell only the important information about the story?		
…write my reactions to what I read? make connections to my life or to situations I know about?		
…ask questions to clarify my curiosity? ….make suggestions or offer solutions?		

Practice Five

For this practice, your story may be in a book, on audio, on a video, or on TV. You will be expected to listen attentively. You might need to listen more than once before you begin writing. Listen to the story that your teacher selects.

Identify: Name the title, the author and publication.
_____
_____

Summarize: Use two to three sentences to summarize the article.
_____
_____
_____

Evaluate: React to what you read. What are your feelings about it?
_____
_____
_____
_____

Question: What questions do you have?
_____
_____

Synthesis: What suggestions do you have?
_____
_____

A new word from your reading: _____

Unit II – Writing in Response to Literary Text
Practice Four

You have had great practice with informational text. For practice 4-6 you will respond to stories or literary text. This is a good time to select a work of fiction. As you summarize think of a beginning, middle, and end.

Identify: Name the title, the author and publication.
_____
_____

Summarize: Use two to three sentences to summarize the article.
_____
_____
_____

Evaluate: React to what you read. What are your feelings about it?
_____
_____
_____
_____

Question: What questions do you have?
_____
_____

Synthesis: What suggestions do you have?
_____
_____

A new word from your reading: _____

Putting it all Together – Assessment 1

Create your own title and write your paragraph

Assessment One

Today, when you write, you will receive an actual grade. This means that you must pay close attention to your rubric, and be sure to double-check your work. Find an article about something or someone unique to where you live. It could be an animal, a person, a building, a custom, or anything that you think makes your city special.

Identify: Name the title, the author and publication.
_____
_____

Summarize: Use two to three sentences to summarize the article.
_____
_____
_____

Evaluate: React to what you read. What are your feelings about it?
_____
_____
_____
_____

Question: What questions do you have?
_____
_____

Synthesis: What suggestions do you have?
_____
_____
_____

A new word from your reading: _____

Vocabulary Check One – Using New Words

Write a story in which you utilize the new words correctly.

Highlight or underline the new words so that your reader may spot them easily.

_____

_____

_____

_____

_____

_____

_____

_____

_____

_____

_____

_____

_____

_____

_____

Vocabulary Check One – New Words

Write your new words. Define them. Write a sentence using each word correctly. Draw a picture that reminds you about the meaning of the word.

Word	Definition	Sentence	Picture
Exhibit	(V) to show or display. (n) a place to display Or show something.	Zoo operators create exhibits to make it easy and safe for visitors to view animals.	

Putting it all Together – Practice 3

Create your own title and write your paragraph

_____

_____
_____
_____
_____
_____
_____
_____
_____
_____
_____
_____
_____
_____

Self-Check: Ask yourself: Did I …	Yes or Not Yet	Teacher
…identify and name the author and title of the article or story?		
…summarize or use two sentences to tell only the important information about the story?		
…write my reactions to what I read? make connections to my life or to situations I know about?		
…ask questions to clarify my curiosity? Make suggestions ….		

Practice Three

Keep practicing. You will get better. Be sure that you are summarizing and not retelling the entire story. Pay attention to the feedback you received and try not to repeat the same mistakes. For this practice, focus on a current event article. It could be a recent story from a newspaper online or in print. The story must be school appropriate.

Identify: Name the title, the author and publication.

_____
_____
_____

Summarize: Use two to three sentences to summarize the article.

_____
_____
_____

Evaluate: React to what you read. What are your feelings about it?

_____
_____
_____
_____

Question: What questions do you have?

_____
_____

Synthesis: What suggestions do you have?

_____
_____

A new word from your reading: _____

Putting it all Together – Practice 2

Create your own title and write your paragraph

_____

_____

_____

_____

_____

_____

_____

_____

_____

_____

_____

_____

_____

Self-Check: Ask yourself: Did I …	Yes, or Not Yet	Teacher
…identify and name the author and title of the article or story?		
…summarize or use two sentences to tell only the important information about the story?		
…write my reactions to what I read? make connections to my life or to situations I know about?		
…ask questions to clarify my curiosity?		
…make suggestions or offer solutions?		

Practice Two

Work on getting better on the aspects you need to improve on. Work to get better every time you write. This time write from an informational article that your teacher or parent selects.

Be sure to follow all the guidelines from page 5 or from the book *Writing to Respond: Cultivating a Habit*.

Identify: Name the title, the author and publication.
_____
_____

Summarize: Use two to three sentences to summarize the article.
_____
_____
_____

Evaluate: React to what you read. What are your feelings about it?
_____
_____
_____
_____

Question: What questions do you have?
_____
_____

Synthesis: What suggestions do you have?
_____
_____

A new word from your reading: _____

Putting it all Together – Practice 1

Create your own title and write your paragraph

_____

_____

_____

_____

_____

_____

_____

_____

_____

_____

_____

_____

_____

Self-Check: Ask yourself: Did I …	Yes or Not Yet	Teacher
…identify and name the author and title of the article or story?		
…summarize or use two sentences to tell only the important information about the story?		
…write my reactions to what I read? make connections to my life or to situations I know about?		
…ask questions to clarify my curiosity? Make suggestions ….		

Unit I – *Writing to Respond* to Informational Text
Practice One

With the help of your teacher or parent, find an article that tells much more about Orangutans, or choose an article about an animal unique to where you live. Read the article, and then write a response using the WTR process. Be sure to select an article that is not too easy or too difficult. Use this graphic organizer to plan.

Identify: Name the title, the author and publication.
_____
_____

Summarize: Use two to three sentences to summarize the article.
_____
_____
_____

Evaluate: React to what you read. What are your feelings about it?
_____
_____
_____
_____

Question: What questions do you have?
_____
_____

Synthesis: What suggestions do you have?
_____
_____

A new word from your reading: _____

Putting it all Together

Now we will put all our responses together in one paragraph.

A Real Home for Orangutans

  The article "Orangutan Escapes from Zoo Exhibit" is written by Tyler Shepard. It is published by clikOrlando.com. The author states that a 7-year-old Orangutan escaped its exhibit from a Kansas City zoo on Sunday July 3, 2016. This incident occurred a few days after an 18-year-old Orangutan escaped from an exhibit at Busch Gardens in Tampa, Florida (Shepard). It is amazing that two Orangutans escaped their exhibits around the same time. Could it be that Orangutans do not like to be held in captivity? I wonder if they are harmful to humans.

  I suggest that Zookeepers be more careful about securing the exhibits that house animals with great climbing skills. Or maybe animals like Orangutans should not be captured. They should be left in the wild where they can climb as high as they wish.

Work Cited

Shepard, T. "Orangutan Escapes from Zoo Exhibit". ClikOrlando.com 4 July 2016.

Student's Model

Identify: Name the title, the author and publication.

The article "Orangutan Escapes from Zoo Exhibit" is written by Tyler Shepard and published by clikOrlando.com

Summarize: Use two to three sentences to summarize the article.

A 7-year-old Orangutan escaped its exhibit from a Kansas City zoo on Sunday July 3, 2016. This incident occurred a few days after an 18-year old Orangutan escaped from an exhibit at Busch Gardens in Tampa (Shepard).

Evaluate: React to what you read. What are your feelings about it?

It is amazing that two Orangutans escaped their exhibits around the same time. Maybe Orangutans do not like being held captive.

Question: What questions do you have?

Are Orangutans harmful to humans?

Synthesis: What suggestions do you have?

Zookeepers should be more careful about securing the exhibits that house animals with great climbing skills. Or maybe animals like Orangutans should not be captured. They should be left in the wild where they can climb as high as they wish.

A new word from reading:_____exhibits_____.

Diagnostic Writing

This exercise is to find out how you will do without practice or examples. Do not worry about mistakes.

Read an article or a story. Write a response to what you read on the following lines.

_____

_____

_____

_____

_____

_____

_____

_____

_____

Teacher's Feedback:

_____

_____

The *Writing to Respond* Rubric

This rubric will be utilized to guide written or oral responses. A copy appears at the bottom of every practice writing page.

Ask yourself these questions: Did I …	Respond: Yes or Not Yet
…identify and name the author and title of the article or story?	
…summarize the article or story? …use two sentences to tell only the important information about the story?	
…write my reactions to what I read? …make connections to my life or to situations I know about?	
…ask questions to clarify my curiosity?	
…make suggestions or try to offer solutions?	

Be sure that your response to each of these questions is "yes" before you submit your assignment.

The *Writing to Respond* (WTR) Process

Utilize the book *Writing to Respond: Cultivating a Habit,* for step-by-step guide and student samples. Take some time to understand the steps in the *Writing to Respond* process, and then with the help of your teacher or parent, begin your first writing practice.

Identify: Name the title, the author and publication.

Summarize: Use two to three sentences to summarize the article.

Evaluate: React to what you read. What are your feelings about it?
Think of the following:

    Do you agree or disagree?

    Are you surprised or sad?

    Can you connect the situation to something you already know?

    What evidence from the article can you use to support your reaction?

Question: What questions do you have?

  Write one question about something that puzzles you or you are curious about.

Synthesis: What suggestions do you have?

    Can you help solve a problem from what you read?

    Do you have a better ending?

    What actions could change the outcomes?

Part 1

Writing to Respond to Text

Informational Text

Literary Text

Multiple Sources

Grades 3-5

    Reflection 36

Part 11 37
    How to Tackle a Test Prompt 38

The Narrative 39
    Narrative Sample Plan. 40
    My Medal for Bravery 41
    Reflect on Quan's Writing 43
    Narrative Writing 45
    Narrative Assessment 47
    Narrative Writing Assessment 48

The Informative Essay 50
    Sample Informative Plan 51
    Informative Writing Practice One: Planning 53
    Informative Writing Practice One: Writing 54
    Informative Writing Practice Two: Planning 56
    Informative Writing Practice Two: Writing 57
    Informative Assessment: Planning 59
    Informative Assessment: Writing 60

The Argument or Opinion 62
    Sample Argument Plan and Writing 63
    Kill them or Not? 65
    Reflection on the Sample Essay 67
    Argument Practice 1: Planning 68
    Argument Practice 1: Writing 69
    Argument Practice 2: Planning 71
    Argument Practice 2: Writing 72
    Argumentative Assessment: Planning 74
    Argumentative Assessment: Writing 75
    Reflection 77

Table of Contents

Part 1 v

The *Writing to Respond* (WTR) Process 1

The *Writing to Respond* Rubric 2

Diagnostic Writing 3

   Unit I – *Writing to Respond* to Informational Text 6

      Practice One 7

      Practice Two 8

      Practice Three 10

      Vocabulary Check One – Using New Words 13

      Assessment One 14

      Putting it all Together – Assessment 1 15

   Unit II – Writing in Response to Literary Text 16

      Practice Four 16

      Putting it all Together – Practice 4 17

      Practice Five 18

      Putting it all Together – Practice 5 19

      Practice Six 20

      Putting it all Together – Practice 6 21

      Vocabulary Check Two – Using New Words 23

      Assessment Two 24

      Putting it all Together – Assessment 2 25

   Unit III – Writing Utilizing Multiple Sources 26

      Practice Seven 26

      Putting it all Together – Practice 7 27

      Practice Eight 28

      Putting it all Together – Practice 8 29

      Practice Nine 30

      Putting it all Together – Practice 9 31

      Vocabulary Check Three – Using New Words 33

      Assessment Three 34

Note to Teachers and Parents

The more time I spend with students, the more convinced I am that all students can succeed. How we determine or discover success in students depend on our level of patience, our willingness to provide them with opportunities to try again and again, and our readiness to take a look at what they have produced even after the due date.

Teachers and parents who have utilized the *Writing to Respond* process as an approach to improve reading and writing skills have testified of the positive effects on students from all groups. This includes, but is not limited to English Language Learners, Exceptional Student Learners, Advanced Placement students, and unmotivated or reluctant learners. Although the path to success for some students might be unconventional, they are all capable of success.

Activities in this workbook are presented in a manner that allows educators or parents to differentiate for students at varying grade levels, with different interest, and diverse learning styles. Teachers can select text with varied complexities and present them in various modalities: print, digital, audio, or audiovisual.

For students who are not yet independent readers, teachers are encouraged to introduce them to the process orally utilizing the 18x24 poster and the individual dry erase 8 ½ x 11 graphic organizers, then gradually proceed to the writing phase.

Help each child succeed! Utilize the *Writing to Respond* process as a tool to guide students on their journey to building writing confidence.

Thank you for utilizing this resource.

Putting it all Together – Practice 5

Create your own title and write your response.

_____

_____

_____

_____

_____

_____

_____

_____

_____

_____

_____

_____

Self-Check: Ask yourself: Did I …	Yes or Not Yet	**Teacher**
…identify and name the author and title of the article or story?		
…summarize or use two sentences to tell only the important information about the story?		
…write my reactions to what I read? make connections to my life or to situations I know about?		
…ask questions to clarify my curiosity? ….make suggestions or offer solutions?		

Practice Six

Read a story that presents a problem or an issue in schools or in cities. Some examples of problems might be poor drinking water, bullying, robbery, mosquito infestation, gangs, or gun violence.

How did the people in the story solve that problem or issue? Can you think of a better solution than the one presented in the story. Write your response in the suggestion section of your response.

Identify: Name the title, the author and publication.
_____
_____

Summarize: Use two to three sentences to summarize the article.
_____
_____
_____

Evaluate: React to what you read. What are your feelings about it?
_____
_____
_____
_____

Question: What questions do you have?
_____
_____

Synthesis: What suggestions do you have?
_____
_____

A new word from your reading: _____

Putting it all Together – Practice 6

Create your own title and write your paragraph

_____

_____

_____

_____

_____

_____

_____

_____

_____

_____

_____

_____

Self-Check: Ask yourself: Did I …	Yes, or Not Yet	Teacher
…identify and name the author and title of the article or story?		
…summarize or use two sentences to tell only the important information about the story?		
…write my reactions to what I read? make connections to my life or to situations I know about?		
…ask questions to clarify my curiosity?		
…make suggestions or offer solutions?		

Vocabulary Check Two – New Words

Write your new words. Define them. Write a sentence using each word correctly. Draw a picture that reminds you about the meaning of the word.

Word	Definition	Sentence	Picture

Vocabulary Check Two – Using New Words

Think about the last fun place you visited, or an imaginary place you would like to visit. Utilize your new words as you tell your story.

Highlight or underline the new words so that your reader may spot them easily.

_____

_____

_____

_____

_____

_____

_____

_____

_____

_____

_____

_____

_____

_____

Assessment Two

At this point, your writing skills should be much improved and you should be very comfortable with the WTR process. For this assessment listen to the story. It will be a work of fiction. Listen attentively. (Teachers modify as needed)

Identify: Name the title, the author and publication.
_____
_____
_____

Summarize: Use two to three sentences to summarize the article.
_____
_____
_____

Evaluate: React to what you read. What are your feelings about it?
_____
_____
_____
_____
_____

Question: What questions do you have?
_____
_____

Synthesis: What suggestions do you have?
_____
_____

A new word from your reading: _____

Putting it all Together – Assessment 2

Create your own title and write your paragraph

_____

_____

_____

_____

_____

_____

_____

_____

_____

_____

_____

_____

Self-Check: Ask yourself: Did I …	Yes, or Not Yet	Teacher
…identify and name the author and title of the article or story?		
…summarize or use two sentences to tell only the important information about the story?		
…write my reactions to what I read? make connections to my life or to situations I know about?		
…ask questions to clarify my curiosity?		
…make suggestions or offer solutions?		

Unit III – Writing Utilizing Multiple Sources
Practice Seven

For practices 7-9, you will utilize multiple sources to find evidence to support your position for or against an issue. Find articles related to a science issue. It could be about genetically modified foods, vaccinations, genetically modified mosquitos, fast foods, or another topic.

Identify: Name the title, the author and publication.
_____
_____

Summarize: Use two to three sentences to summarize the article.
_____
_____
_____

Evaluate: React to what you read. What is your opinion on the issue?
_____
_____
_____
_____

Question: What questions do you have?
_____
_____

Synthesis: What suggestions do you have?
_____
_____

A new word from your reading: _____

Putting it all Together – Practice 7

Create your own title and write your paragraph

_____

_____

_____

_____

_____

_____

_____

_____

_____

_____

_____

_____

Self-Check: Ask yourself: Did I ...	Yes, or Not Yet	Teacher
...identify and name the author and title of the article or story?		
...summarize or use two sentences to tell only the important information about the story?		
...write my reactions to what I read? make connections to my life or to situations I know about?		
...ask questions to clarify my curiosity?		
...make suggestions or offer solutions?		

Practice Eight

Find articles related to a social studies issue. It could be about migration, war, diseases, developing cities, cheating in sports, or anything that you and your teacher or parents choose.

Identify: Name the title, the author and publication.
_____
_____

Summarize: Use two to three sentences to summarize the article.
_____
_____
_____

Evaluate: React to what you read. How would you defend a decision on that issue?
_____
_____
_____
_____

Question: What questions do you have?
_____
_____

Synthesis: What suggestions do you have?
_____
_____

A new word from your reading: _____

Putting it all Together – Practice 8

Create your own title and write your paragraph

___

Self-Check: Ask yourself: Did I …	Yes, or Not Yet	Teacher
…identify and name the author and title of the article or story?		
…summarize or use two sentences to tell only the important information about the story?		
…write my reactions to what I read? make connections to my life or to situations I know about?		
…ask questions to clarify my curiosity?		
…make suggestions or offer solutions?		

Practice Nine

Find three sources about a topic. Each source should be different. It could be a written article, picture, video, or audio. Write your response. Remember to use evidence from two or more of the sources to support your reaction.

Identify: Name the title, the author and publication.
_____
_____

Summarize: Use two to three sentences to summarize the article.
_____
_____
_____

Evaluate: React to what you read. What evidence can you find to support your reaction?
_____
_____
_____
_____
_____

Question: What questions do you have?
_____
_____

Synthesis: What suggestions do you have?
_____
_____

A new word from your reading: _____

Putting it all Together – Practice 9

Create your own title and write your paragraph

_____

_____

_____

_____

_____

_____

_____

_____

_____

_____

_____

_____

_____

Self-Check: Ask yourself: Did I ...	Yes, or Not Yet	Teacher
...identify and name the author and title of the article or story?		
...summarize or use two sentences to tell only the important information about the story?		
...write my reactions to what I read? make connections to my life or to situations I know about?		
...ask questions to clarify my curiosity?		
...make suggestions or offer solutions?		

Vocabulary Check three – New Words

Write your new words. Define them. Write a sentence using each word correctly. Draw a picture that reminds you about the meaning of the word.

Word	Definition	Sentence	Picture

Vocabulary Check Three – Using New Words

Think about the last fun place you visited or an imaginary place you would like to visit. Utilize your new words as you tell your story.

Be sure to use the words correctly. Highlight or underline the new words so that your reader may spot them easily.

_____

_____

_____

_____

_____

_____

_____

_____

_____

_____

_____

_____

_____

Assessment Three

Congratulations! You have completed several practices and you should be on your way to becoming a confident writer. For this assessment you will read and write to respond utilizing multiple sources.

Identify: Name the title, the author and publication.
_____
_____
_____

Summarize: Use two to three sentences to summarize the article.
_____
_____
_____
_____

Evaluate: React to what you read. How would you justify or challenge the main concern presented in the sources?
_____
_____
_____
_____
_____

Question: What questions do you have?
_____
_____

Synthesis: What suggestions do you have?
_____
_____
_____

A new word from your reading: _____

Putting it all Together – Assessment 3

Create your own title and write your paragraph

_____

_____

_____

_____

_____

_____

_____

_____

_____

_____

_____

_____

_____

Self-Check: Ask yourself: Did I …	Yes, or Not Yet	Teacher
…identify and name the author and title of the article or story?		
…summarize or use two sentences to tell only the important information about the story?		
…write my reactions to what I read? make connections to my life or to situations I know about?		
…ask questions to clarify my curiosity?		
…make suggestions or offer solutions?		

Reflection

This is time to reflect on your growth as a writer.

_____
_____
_____
_____
_____
_____
_____

Your Teacher's Overall feedback on your development as a writer

_____
_____
_____
_____
_____
_____

Part 11

Writing to Respond to Test Prompts

Narrative

Informative

Argumentative or Opinion

Grades 3-5

NB. The rubrics created for this document align with Common Core writing specifications and reflect elements of Smarter Balanced Consortiums scoring guide.

Works Cited

Joseph Watts, *Writing to Respond to Text and Tests.* USA. 2015. Print

"Smarter Balanced English/Language Arts Scoring Guide Grades 3-5. Smarter Balanced Consortium. 10 Oct. 2014. Web. 19 July 2016.

How to Tackle a Test Prompt

Read - read the prompt

Identify - identify the important words

Determine – determine the kind of writing based on the key words

Plan - utilize a graphic organizer that best suits the kind of writing

Write – follow your plan

Double-check – go over your work. Look for errors in conventions

Read the prompt before reading anything else. While you read, underline key words that will help you understand the writing task. Based on the key words you will be able to determine if you are being asked to tell a story, explain an idea, or give an opinion. Once you've figured out the task, pick a suitable graphic organizer to help you plan your writing.

This is the time to read or listen to all sources that will help you plan your essay. Formulate your ideas and extract evidence from your sources to help you create a good plan. It is a good idea to paraphrase or put the evidence into your own words.

Now you are ready to write your test response. Be sure to follow your plan. Use transitional words to connect your ideas. Elaborate or tell more about your evidence. Use Standard English. Pay attention to the use of words that relate to your topic. Use punctuations and grammar correctly. Spell words correctly. Keep your allotted time in mind.

Always double-check your work before you end your test.

The Narrative

The narrative tells a story. The narrator or the person telling the story must have a reason or a point for telling the story.

The point of the story can also be the moral or lesson learned from the experience.

A narrative can be written from different points of views.

If the narrator uses "I" while telling the story it means that the story is being told form the first person.

If the narrator uses "we" while telling a story, it means that the narrator and other people are part of the story.

When the narrator or person telling the story uses "they, he, and she" this means that he or she is not part of the story. He or she is telling the story as an onlooker.

When preparing to tell a narrative, think of an experience and a reason or the point for telling the story. Think of a beginning, a middle and an end.

A narrative test prompt may ask to tell about an experience, about someone you admire, or about something you believe.

Example

Before reading the prompt, allow students to read one or more of these stories: *A Sick Day for Amos McGee* by Phillip and Erin Stead, (K-2), or *Kindness is Cooler, Mr. Ruller,* by Margery Cuyler, (k-5), or *Ordinary Mary's Extra Ordinary Deed*, Emily Pearson

Prompt

Read the stories about people helping others or being helped. Then write a story about a time when you helped someone, **or** when someone was helpful to you. You can use the stories as points of comparisons. While you plan, focus on a beginning, a middle and an end. Utilize a graphic organizer to plan your work

Narrative Sample Plan.

Aspects of Narrative	Details for my Narrative

Beginning:
   Place
   Time
   Who
   The problem to be solved
	At the community center's swimming pool
	One afternoon during the last week of summer
	my little cousin Alec
	Alec was drowning and needed to be rescued

Middle The series of events to solve the problems	I jumped into the pool, swam to where Alec was, approached him from the back and pulled him up
End How did it end? The solution to the problem	I managed to get to pool-side. An adult performed CPR. Alec coughed and recovered. One week later I was rewarded.
Point My reason for telling the story. The moral or the lesson learned	Serve well. You can save a life in the process. A good reward is also welcoming.

My Medal for Bravery

Summer is one of the best times of the year for my brothers, cousins, friends, and me. Every year, during the last week of summer we look forward to shopping for school, and the back to school event at the community center. This year was no different. We shopped for the cool things we wanted for school, and then came the best part, our swimming pool day. It was the most exciting day of our summer vacation.

Our big day was always the last Friday before the start of school. Parents brought hot dogs, ham burgers, chicken, marshmallows, and drinks. The day was bright and perfect for the occasion. By 11 o'clock the pool was colorful. Bright colored swim wear and floating devices were everywhere. Before we knew it, it was lunch time, and the loud chattering of exited students had subsided.

One hour after lunch, we went back into the water. About fifteen minutes into our afternoon swimming, I heard an odd sound to my right. I turned in time to see my four-year-old cousin, Alec, bopping up and down in the water.

"He...lp! Heeep, hhhh, heeee"

I thought of the rule we learned at junior firefighter's camp: "Reach, throw, row, don't go". But I had to act now and fast. I jumped into the pool and swam towards Alec. I approached him from the back, dove beneath him, and hoisted him upwards. By that time, Alec's mom, my aunt Riz, had noticed and dove into the pool to help. After coughing out much water, Alec was dazed, and confused, but alive.

Those who witnessed the incident blurted comments like, "He is a hero". "He is really brave". "Bearly eleven and he thinks so quickly".

I did not feel heroic. I simply helped when it mattered most.

At school, everyone spoke about the incident. Just when I thought it was time to move on, something really surprising occurred. On the Friday of that week, as I headed to lunch, I noticed that there were parents and more adults than usual at school. As I entered the cafeteria, I heard a burst of deafening cheers. "Hurrah, bravo, to our young hero, Quan Roche".

I did not know that our local firefighters had organized a ceremony to present me with a medal for bravery. I was overwhelmed with surprise. I thought, if at eleven I can make so many people happy, I won't stop helping others.

Reflect on Quan's Writing

React to the beginning, middle and end?

_____

_____

_____

_____

What is the point or reason for telling the story? Is there a lesson?

_____

_____

_____

_____

Can you find examples of dialogue?

_____

_____

How can you tell that Quan is the narrator of the story?

_____

Narrative Practice 1

Write your own story about a time you helped someone. Use the graphic organizer provided.

Aspects of Narrative	Details for my Narrative
Beginning: Place Time Who The problem to be solved	
Middle: The series of events to solve the problems	
End: How did it end? The solution to the problem	
Point: My reason for telling the Story. The moral or the lesson learned	

Narrative Writing

Follow the plan you created and write your narrative.

_____

Narrative Assessment

Prompt

Read the stories about important people in history. Then write a story about a person you admire. The person may be a relative, an athlete, an actress/actor, a politician or someone who has had a special impact on you. Be sure to focus on a beginning, a middle and an end. Utilize a graphic organizer to plan your work.

Aspects of Narrative	Details for my Narrative
Beginning: Place Time Who The problem to be solved	
Middle: The series of events to solve the problems	
End: How did it end? The solution to the problem	
Point: My reason for telling the Story. The moral or the lesson learned	

Narrative Writing

Follow the plan you created and write your narrative.

The Informative Essay

Informative writing focuses mainly on informing the reader. The writer may be asked to explain an idea, compare one thing or idea to another, or give reasons for the cause or effect on something.

- Words like explain, and inform mean that the writer should focus on writing an explanation.
- Words like similar, different, and compare mean that the writer should focus on comparing two ideas.
- Words like reason, cause, and effect mean that the writer will write about how something affects another.

Reading the prompt carefully will help you determine what kind of informative writing to focus on.

Prompt

Read the following articles about the history of ice-cream. Write an essay in which you explain to your peers how the recipe for ice-cream evolved or changed over centuries. Be sure to utilize information from the sources you read. Cite your sources adequately.

Source 1: The History of Ice Cream from the Old Farmer's Almanac

Source 2: YouTube video Ice-cream History

Sample Informative Plan

Main Points	Explanation and evidence to support
Introduction **Thesis**	Background Main idea: the main ingredients used to make ice cream changed as it was introduced to different countries
Point one **Details** **Source 1**	BC Rome, China, - mixed nectar and fruits with snow, and served to kings, and important people Heated fermented milk, flour and camphor
Point two **Details** **Source**	Italy, France, England- mixed flour, water, honey, milk with ice, for the wealthy stir while freezing
Point three **Details** **Source 3**	America- cream, a churn and ice-cream factory milk, cream, sugar, vanilla, churn, flavored : churned, waffle cones
Conclusion	the concept remains, but people still substitute ingredients to suit their taste or customers' needs

Amazing Journey: Thank You

Ice-cream is one of my favorite desserts. I am almost certain that most of us who grin from ear to ear when we hear the word ice-cream never think about how it came to be. Everything has a history, and the recipe for ice-cream is no different.

According to source 1, the idea of ice-cream was around from as early as the BCs in Rome. It was a strange mix of snow, and nectar. And sadly, it was only served to kings and other important people in their court or palace.

Thankfully, in the thirteenth century when Marco Polo returned from his trip to the Far East he brought the idea of ice-cream to Italy (Source 2). Even then, it did not look like what we eat today, and it was still only served to kings and queens. According to Source 2, it consisted of a heated fermented milk, flour, and camphor mixed with ice.

Source 1 states by the time ice-cream was introduced to France and England by royal families from Italy, it was made from a mixture of milk, cream, butter and eggs. The ingredients were stirred while freezing. This recipe is closer to what we use today,

Finally, in the sixteen hundreds when the early Europeans migrated to America, they brought the idea of ice-cream with them. According to Source 2, the main ingredients were milk, sugar and flavoring, mainly vanilla. Because ice was not very common, it was difficult to produce ice-cream for ordinary people. It was a favorite for presidents, and wealthy people.

I'm happy to know that in the 1800s when ice became more readily available, Americans transformed ice-cream. The recipe changed to include mainly cream. A factory for ice-cream became a brilliant idea, and soon everyone, including soldiers at war could enjoy ice-cream (Source 3). Today the main ingredients are still cream, milk, sweeteners, and flavorings, but ingredients can be substituted to suit taste and health needs. After so many centuries, ice-cream is still a favorite delicacy. We are happy that ice-cream can be enjoyed by everyone including children.

Informative Writing Practice One: Planning

With the help of a teacher or parent find three different sources that provide information about the history of something phenomenal or special. You can think of a sport, a custom, a food, or even a practice like attending school. Then write an explanatory essay in which you inform your audience about your findings. Be sure to utilize information from all your sources.

Main Points	Explanation and evidence to support
Introduction **Thesis**	
Point one Details Source	
Point two Details Source	
Point three Details Source	
Conclusion	

Informative Writing Practice One: Writing

Follow your plan, and write your essay.

Informative Writing Practice Two: Planning

With your teacher or parent decide on a topic that you would like to write about. Find at least three sources. Sources may be a video clip, an article or an image. Write an explanatory essay in which you inform your audience about your findings.

Main Points	Explanation and evidence to support
Introduction **Thesis**	

Point one
 	
    Details
 	
    Source	

Point two
 	
    Details
 	
    Source	

Point three
 	
    Details
 	
    Source	

Conclusion	

Informative Writing Practice Two: Writing

Follow your plan, and write your essay.

Informative Assessment: Planning

Introduction **Thesis**	

Point one
    Details
 	
    Source	

Point two
    Details
 	
    Source	

Point three
    Details
 	
    Source	

Conclusion	

Informative Assessment: Writing

Follow your plan, and write your essay.

The Argument or Opinion

The opinion or argument takes a side on an issue. The writer must provide a reason for supporting the issue, and provide evidence to support the reasons. The writer must mention the opposing view, and refute or let readers know why the opposing view should not be supported.

The aim is to stick to one position to the end. There is no need to support both sides, or to change position halfway through the writing.

Although an introduction and a conclusion are important aspects of the essay, the claim, reasons, evidence, opposing claim and refutation of the opposing claim are the most important.

Always remember to present evidence carefully. This means paraphrase or put the evidence in your own words and say and cite the source. Work on integrating the evidence into the writing. This can be achieved by utilizing evidence to support the position, and then elaborating on what the evidence suggests. Always read the prompt first. This will create a purpose for reading the sources.

Prompt

Wild animals like bears, and alligators are known for mauling or killing humans. In most cases the animals are euthanized or killed. Some people support the idea while others oppose it. Read the sources provided, and then write an essay in which you present your opinion or argument for or against the killing of animals after they attack humans. Be sure to utilize evidence from the sources provided to support your position.

Brulliard, Karin. "Should Wild Animals that Attack People be Killed? The Washington Post, 27 June 2016. 24 July 2016

Landers, Jackson. "Why Kill Animals that Attack Humans?" Science. The State of the Universe 11 July 2012. 24 July 2-16.

Sample Argument Plan and Writing

Should animals be killed after they harm humans?

For /yes/ pro	Against/ no/ con
• To prevent future attacks by that animal • To make the family of the victims feel better • To prevent retaliation from friends of the victim	• Animals only harm humans when they feel threatened • It is natural for animals to attack humans

Ideas for Introduction: Humans and animals have struggled over sharing the same space.

Thesis = Claim + reasons

Wild animals that attack humans should be killed <u>to prevent future attacks, to comfort the victim's family, and to prevent widespread killing of the animals.</u>

Point one	Paraphrased evidence/ source
• To prevent future attacks by that animal **Evidence** 'predators usually exhibit repeat behavior" **Source** 1	When predators enjoyed their first experience, they usually return. Killing the animal will prevent more deaths.

Point two • To comfort family of the victims, and treat victims where possible. **Evidence directly from source** New Mexico… "Laws require them to euthanize and test wild animals that attack or bite a person,"… Source 1 **Point Three** After Steve Irwin's death by a stingray, angry supporters killed thousands of stingrays. Source 2	**Paraphrased evidence/ source** In New Mexico they capture, kill, and test any wild animal that attacks humans. They do that to ensure that the animal was not infected with diseases that can infect the person attacked. It prevents angry people from killing more animals than they should.
Opposing Claim natural for them to behave that way " people decried ….animal was acting defensively" bare was startled source 1	People should not startle or roam where these animals live.
Refutation National park ranger states that bears usually stay in their quarters. If they attack humans they need to be killed Source	**Paraphrased evidence/ source** National park rangers believe that although bears are predators, attacking humans is unacceptable and should be killed when they do.
Conclusion :	There are fair reasons why animals that attack humans should be killed.

Kill them or Not?

Humans and animals have struggled over sharing the same space for centuries. There are many heroic stories of man winning his fight with wild animals. However, there have been countless stories of wild animals mauling or killing humans even in areas close to homes. People disagree on whether these animals should be killed. **Wild animals that attack humans should be killed** to prevent future attacks, to comfort the victim's family, and to prevent widespread killing of the animal.

According to source 2 animal predators that attack humans will usually do it again. It's like a bear or a monkey returning for human food left out in the open. These animals wander to where people live and attack them repeatedly. Therefore, the best way to prevent other attacks on innocent humans is to kill the animal.

Another reason for killing animals that attack humans is that it brings comfort to the grieving family or victim. A lion killed a boy while he was playing in his yard, and an alligator harmed a woman while she was swimming (Source 1). Both animals were killed and the family of the victims were pleased. When the victim does not die, there is the concern of diseases like rabies. According to source 1, in New Mexico they capture, kill, and test any wild animal that attacks humans. This practice is to make sure they provide the right treatment to the victim. Animals like bears carry diseases like rabies. If the animal is captured and tested, then the victim can be treated to prevent death. This practice is fair.

In addition to concerns for the family and victim, there is also concern for the survival of the animal species. According to source 2, when wild animals kill a human, angry hunters go after any animal of its kind and can kill many of these animals still not knowing if they killed the correct one. One example is after the death of Steve Irwin by a stingray, thousands of stingrays were killed. The same happened in an African rural village when a lion killed a human. If the anger displayed by these people can be lessened by killing the accused animal, then this might be the best solution.

Those who do not support the killing of animals that attack humans state that the animals are usually in their habitat and humans may have attacked or startled them (Source 1). National park rangers believe that though animals like bears are predators, it is abnormal for bears to hunt humans as prey and should be killed when they develop the habit.

The case for killing wild animals that attack people is fair. We continue to read stories of animals attacking or killing humans in places that humans should feel protected. To prevent the repeat behavior, and human outrage these attackers must be killed.

Reflection on the Sample Essay

Make notes on aspects of the sample argument.

Argument Practice 1: Planning

Pick a topic that presents opposing views. It could be an issue or idea that you feel passionate about. It could be a school issue. With the help of your teacher or parent, find three sources that present varying views on the topic. Then write an essay in which you present your position on the topic. Be sure to utilize information from the sources to support your position. Utilize the graphic organizer to plan your work.

For /yes/ pro	Against/ no/ con
Ideas for Introduction: Thesis = Claim + reasons	
Point one **Evidence** **Source**	Paraphrased evidence/ source
Point two **Evidence** **Source**	Paraphrased evidence/ source
Opposing Claim	
Refutation **Source**	Paraphrased evidence/ source
Conclusion	

Argument Practice 1: Writing

Follow your plan, and write your essay.

Argument Practice 2: Planning

Pick a topic that presents opposing views. It could be an issue or idea that you feel passionate about. It could be a school issue. With the help of your teacher or parent, find three sources that present varying views on the topic. Then write an essay in which you present your position on the topic. Be sure to utilize information from the sources to support your position. Utilize the graphic organizer to plan your work.

For /yes/ pro	Against/ no/ con
Ideas for Introduction: **Thesis = Claim + reasons**	
Point one **Evidence** **Source**	Paraphrased evidence/ source
Point two **Evidence** **Source**	Paraphrased evidence/ source
Opposing Claim	
Refutation **Source**	Paraphrased evidence/ source
Conclusion	

Argument Practice 2: Planning

Pick a topic that presents opposing views. It could be an issue or idea that you feel passionate about. It could be a school issue. With the help of your teacher or parent, find three sources that present varying views on the topic. Then write an essay in which you present your position on the topic. Be sure to utilize information from the sources to support your position. Utilize the graphic organizer to plan your work.

For /yes/ pro	Against/ no/ con
Ideas for Introduction: **Thesis = Claim + reasons**	
Point one **Evidence** **Source**	Paraphrased evidence/ source
Point two **Evidence** **Source**	Paraphrased evidence/ source
Opposing Claim	
Refutation **Source**	Paraphrased evidence/ source
Conclusion	

Argument Practice 2: Writing

Follow your plan, and write your essay.

Argumentative Assessment: Planning

This exercise will test your ability to write an opinion paper without help. You will be given three sources that present varying views on the topic. Read the prompt. Utilize the resources wisely. Find evidence to support your position. Paraphrase the evidence. Utilize the graphic organizer to plan your work. Write with confidence.

For /yes/ pro	Against/ no/ con
Ideas for Introduction: Thesis = Claim + reasons	
Point one Evidence Source	Paraphrased evidence/ source
Point two Evidence Source	Paraphrased evidence/ source
Opposing Claim	
Refutation Source	Paraphrased evidence/ source
Conclusion	

Argumentative Assessment: Writing

Follow your plan, and write your essay.

_____

_____
_____
_____
_____
_____
_____
_____
_____
_____
_____
_____
_____
_____

Reflection

Reflect on your journey as a writer for the school year.

_____

_____
_____
_____
_____
_____
_____
_____
_____
_____
_____
_____
_____
_____

Narrative Rubric by Joseph Watts 2016

Categories	3	2	Not Yet: Does not meet standards
Purpose- The reason for writing the essay The essay does exactly what it says it will do from the start to the end. It tells a story that presents a lesson or moral	There is a clearly stated thesis. The writer utilizes clear details to convey the message in a progressive manner.	There is a guiding sentence that serves as a thesis. The story progresses well, but there is no point or reason for telling the story	There is no clear thesis. Events do not follow a plot. There is no point or reason for the story.
Organization -The order in which the paragraphs are presented in the essay The paragraphs are organized to suit the writing style, and they flow very well from paragraph to paragraph. Presents a beginning, a middle and an end. There is a point or reason for telling the story.	There is a suitable introduction. It includes the thesis, and points are presented in a consistent story telling style. Characters develop realistically. Direct quotes and transitional words are used to effectively connect elements of the story.	There is a suitable introduction. It includes the thesis, and points are presented in a consistent story telling style. Characters develop realistically. Lacks the use of direct quotes and transitional words to effectively connect elements of the story.	There is no introduction. The paragraphs are presented in a confusing manner. The writing does not follow the writing style.
Pacing: The story paces the story in a realistic and believable manner The writer uses effective transitional words to pace the story. The writers utilizes descriptive words that bring characters and events to life.	The writer introduces events in a steady, suitable, and realistic manner while conveying the message.	The writer introduces in a sequential manner, but plot is simple, predictable, and progresses too quickly or too slowly.	The writer tells a group of events not well connected to each other. Story is confusing.
Point: The lesson, message, or moral portrayed in the story. The writer uses clear language to present the details that convey the message or lesson of the story.	The writer utilizes effective vocabulary to present the ideas, and reason or point for telling the story.	The writer presents the ideas, and reason or point for telling the story, but does not utilize the best vocabulary for the writing style.	The writer presents a group of events that are poorly connected. There is no point or reason for telling the story.
Conventions-The way the writer uses grammar, spells, and punctuates sentences. The writer demonstrates a good command of conventions.	The writer constructs correct sentences that follow rules of grammar, usage, punctuation, spelling, and capitalization.	The writer has three or more errors in conventions.	The writer has five or more errors in several areas of conventions.
Style- The way a writer sounds when responding to a specific writing style The writer uses clear sentences, and utilizes point of view, and pronoun antecedents correctly. There is also a strong sense of finality.	The voice suits the writing style. The point of view is steady. Pronoun antecedents are correctly utilized. The tone is formal, the purpose is clearly communicated, and there is a strong sense of finality.	The voice is clear and predominantly formal, but there are one to three errors in one or more of these areas: shift in point of view, pronoun-antecedent agreement, and wordiness. The story ends well.	The writer changes point of view. The writer uses the second person point of view. Sentences are wordy and unclear. The story lacks finality.

Modified Rubric for Informative Essay from *Writing to Respond to Text and Tests*. Joseph Watts 2015

Categories	3	2	Not Yet: Does not meet standards
Purpose- The reason for writing the essay	The thesis statement is clear. The thesis is supported with good points.	The thesis clear. Supporting points are inadequate. The writer does not provide sufficient details to support the thesis.	The thesis statement is not clear. There is no thesis statement, and the writing is confusing. There are no details to support the thesis.
Organization -The order in which the paragraphs are presented in the essay	There is a suitable introduction. It includes a thesis statement. The points in the thesis are developed in paragraphs in the order presented. Transitions are used effectively to connect paragraphs. There is a strong conclusion.	There is an introduction that includes a thesis statement. The points are developed in paragraphs in the order presented in the thesis. There are no transitions. There is no conclusion.	There is no introduction. The paragraphs are presented in a confusing manner and do not follow the writing style.
Evidence- The way the writer supports what he or she states in the essay	The writer introduces evidence correctly and uses correct citation. There is a balance between paraphrased and direct quotations.	The writer introduces evidence, but does not paraphrase, and does not cite correctly.	The writer utilizes sources, but copies directly from the text with no citation. The writer does not utilize sources.
Elaboration- The way the writer explains or clarifies a point or evidence	The writer uses the best vocabulary words that suit the writing style to present and explain the evidence.	The writer presents evidence, explains and elaborates, but does not use best vocabulary for the writing style.	The writer presents evidence but does not explain or elaborate. The writer does not present evidence.
Conventions-The way the writer uses grammar, spells, and punctuates sentences	The writer uses clear language to present the evidence, explains well, and elaborates where necessary. The writer constructs correct sentences that follow rules of grammar, usage, punctuation, spelling, and capitalization.	The writer has three or more errors in conventions.	The writer has five or more errors in several areas of conventions. Grammar, punctuation, spelling etc.
Style- The way a writer sounds when responding to a specific writing style	The writer demonstrates a good command of conventions. The voice suits the writing style. The point of view is steady. Pronoun antecedents are correctly utilized. The tone is formal, the purpose is clearly communicated, and there is a strong sense of finality.	The voice is clear and predominantly formal, but there are one to three errors in one or more of these areas: shift in point of view, pronoun-antecedent agreement, and wordiness. The essay ends well.	The writer changes point of view. The writer uses the second person point of view. Sentences are wordy and unclear.
	The writer uses clear sentences, and utilizes point of view, and pronoun antecedents correctly. There is also a strong sense of finality.		

The essay does exactly what it says it will do from the start to the end. It informs or explains.

Present a thesis, supporting points and details to support the points.

Modified Rubric for Argumentative Essay from *Writing to Respond to Text and Tests*. Joseph Watts 2015

Categories	3	2	Not Yet: Does not meet standards
Purpose- The reason for writing the essay The essay does exactly what it says it will do from the start to the end. It argues a point/takes a position and defends it.	There is a clearly stated claim. The claim is supported by reasons. The writer sticks to his/her opinion till the end.	The claim is clear. Reasons are inadequate. The writer does not sustain or stick to the claim to the end.	The claim is not clear, or There is no claim, and the writing is a ramble. There are no reasons to support the claim.
Organization -The order in which the paragraphs are presented in the essay The paragraphs are organized to suit the writing style, and they flow very well from paragraph to paragraph. The writer presents a claim, supports the claim with reasons, presents and refutes the opposing claim, and concludes with confidence.	There is a suitable introduction. It includes the claim, and reasons or support for the claim. The reasons are developed in paragraphs in the order presented. The writer presents and refutes the opposing claim and concludes. Transitions are used to connect paragraphs.	There is an introduction that includes a claim and reasons. The reasons are developed in paragraphs in the order presented. The writer presents but does not refute the opposing claim, and may have at least one area lacking.	There is no introduction. The paragraphs are presented in a confusing manner. The writing does not follow the writing style.
Evidence- The way the writer supports what he or she states in the essay The writer extracts evidence from sources, paraphrases and utilizes the evidence effectively, and uses proper in-text citation to acknowledge the author's work.	The writer introduces evidence correctly and uses correct citation. There is a balance between paraphrased and direct quotations.	The writer introduces evidence but does not paraphrase and does not cite correctly.	The writer utilizes sources, but copies directly from the text with no citation. The writer does not utilize sources.
Elaboration- The way the writer explains or clarifies a point or evidence The writer uses clear language to present the evidence, explains well, and elaborates where necessary.	The writer uses the best vocabulary words that suit the writing style to present and explain the evidence.	The writer presents evidence and explains and elaborates, but does not use the best vocabulary for the writing style.	The writer presents evidence but does not explain or elaborate. The writer does not present evidence.
Conventions-The way the writer uses grammar, spells, and punctuates sentences The writer demonstrates a good command of conventions.	The writer constructs correct sentences that follow rules of grammar, usage, punctuation, spelling, and capitalization.	The writer has three or more errors in conventions.	The writer has five or more errors in several areas of conventions. Grammar, punctuation, spelling etc.
Style- The way a writer sounds when responding to a specific writing style The writer uses clear sentences, and utilizes point of view, and pronoun antecedents correctly. There is also a strong sense of finality.	The voice suits the writing style. The point of view is steady. Pronoun antecedents are correctly utilized. The tone is formal, the purpose is clearly communicated, and there is a strong sense of finality.	The voice is clear and predominantly formal, but there are one to three errors in one or more of these areas: shift in point of view, pronoun-antecedent agreement, and wordiness. The essay ends well.	The writer changes point of view. The writer uses the second person point of view. Sentences are wordy and unclear. The essay does not have an end.

Write to Win!

Read frequently.

Read informational text.

Read literary text. Learn new words.

Write responses every time you read.

Be sure that the reading is not too easy or too difficult.

Always find out the title and author of the story you are reading.

Write summaries and then write reactions.

Ask questions. Solve problems. Take sides. Devise plans.

Challenge opinions, and use evidence to support your position.

Think and then write your thoughts with confidence.

Other *Writing to Respond* Resources

 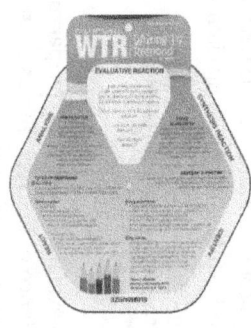 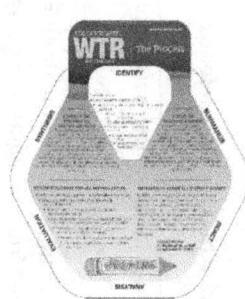

www.ingramcontent.com/pod-product-compliance
Lightning Source LLC
Chambersburg PA
CBHW081122080526
44587CB00021B/3712